DC SECRETS REVEALED!

BEHIND THE SCENES WITH Harley Quinn™

by Steve Korté

Batman created by Bob Kane with Bill Finger
Harley Quinn created by Paul Dini and Bruce Timm

raintree
a Capstone company — publishers for children

Raintree is an imprint of Capstone Global Library Limited, a company incorporated in England and Wales having its registered office at 264 Banbury Road, Oxford, OX2 7DY – Registered company number: 6695582

www.raintree.co.uk
myorders@raintree.co.uk

Copyright © 2025 DC.
BATMAN and all related characters and elements © & ™ DC. (s25)

All rights reserved. No part of this publication may be reproduced in any form or by any means (including photocopying or storing it in any medium by electronic means and whether or not transiently or incidentally to some other use of this publication) without the written permission of the copyright owner, except in accordance with the provisions of the Copyright, Designs and Patents Act 1988 or under the terms of a licence issued by the Copyright Licensing Agency, 5th Floor, Shackleton House, 4 Battle Bridge Lane, London SE1 2HX (www.cla.co.uk). Applications for the copyright owner's written permission should be addressed to the publisher.

ISBN 978 1 3982 5697 2 (hardback)

Editorial Credits
Edited by Christopher Harbo
Designed by Sarah Bennett
Production by Katy LaVigne
Printed and bound in India

Acknowledgements
We would like to thank the following for permission to reproduce photographs: Design Elements and Images by Shutterstock/delcarmat, 8 (harlequin), Shutterstock/Denys_kh (diamond background), 8, 14–15, 18–19, Shutterstock/mei yanotai (folder), 22, 26, 28, Shutterstock/Vickey Chauhan (hyena), 17 (top)

British Library Cataloguing in Publication Data
A full catalogue record for this book is available from the British Library.

Contents

Meet Harley Quinn 4

The name is Quinn, Harley Quinn! 6

Harlequin vs Harley Quinn 8

Tools of the trade 10

The Joker 12

Dear Puddin' 14

Giggles and Crackers 16

The many skills of Harley Quinn 18

Horrible heroes 20

Best friends . . . forever? 24

Friends or foes? 26

    Historical highlights of the
    Clown Princess of Crime 30

    About the author 32

Meet Harley Quinn

What kind of wacky person would dedicate her life to working with The Joker?

The answer is simple: Harley Quinn!

Harley started out as The Joker's assistant, happily helping him torment Batman. She would do anything if it earned even the smallest smile from the Clown Prince of Crime.

But Harley soon had big plans of her own. After several years with The Joker, she launched a solo career as Gotham City's Clown Princess of Crime. Now she sometimes teams up with other villains. Every now and again, she even tries to give up her life of crime.

But something always seems to drag her back to the wrong side of the law.

Notable quotes of Harley Quinn

"At what point did my life go looney tunes?"

"I got me some powers, baby!"

"We now resume our regularly scheduled pummelling!"

The name is Quinn, Harley Quinn!

Harleen Quinzel was a psychiatrist who graduated at the top of her class at Gotham University. Her first job was at a hospital, but she soon became interested in studying the criminal mind. She moved her practice to Arkham Asylum.

At Arkham, Dr Quinzel conducted private sessions with The Joker. She found him to be as charming as he was criminal. Her admiration for him became so intense, she helped him to escape. Then she transformed herself into Harley Quinn to follow in The Joker's demented footsteps!

Harlequin vs Harley Quinn

When Harleen Quinzel chose a costume for her life of crime, she was inspired by the harlequin of long ago. No one knows exactly when the first harlequin appeared, but the character showed up in Italian theatre performances during the 16th century. Usually a man, the harlequin was a lighthearted servant who caused all kinds of trouble for his employer. The harlequin also loved to play silly tricks on people.

Fun facts about harlequins

They often had shaved heads.

They sometimes carried wooden swords.

They wore black masks because the colour was associated with trickery.

In Britain, Harlequins starred in pantomime plays known as harlequinades.

For centuries, children watched puppet shows where a harlequin fought with a character called Punchinello.

Did you know?

Before Harley arrived in Gotham City, four other female villains used the name Harlequin.

- The first Harlequin was Molly Mayne, who caused problems for Green Lantern.

- The second Harlequin was a woman called Duela Dent, who pretended to be The Joker's daughter.

- The third Harlequin was Marcie Cooper, who worked at the same office as Molly Mayne.

- The fourth Harlequin was a mysterious woman who could work magic. Her real identity was never revealed.

Trouble? Don't mind if I do!

Tools of the trade

Batman and his fellow heroes wear Utility Belts filled with top-of-the-range crime-fighting tools. Harley Quinn has a gag bag. It contains the wackiest and wildest crime-causing and mischief-making tools!

My gag bag full of stuff is like your Utility Belt, only way more fun!

Whoopee Cushion Don't look now, but Harley just slipped one of her custom-made, red-and-black whoopee cushions under her foe before she sat down! **BRAAAP!**

Sneezing Powder Harley's extra-strength sneezing powder causes people to sneeze uncontrollably.

Glitter Bombs When Harley detonates her glitter bombs, the explosion completely covers her foes in tiny, shiny flakes.

Sticky String Harley's sticky strings are perfect for tying up her foes. As the gooey strands wrap up her opponents, Harley makes her escape – unless a pesky Super Hero has something to say about it.

Stink Bombs Harley's stink bombs can clear a room in seconds. The smell is similar to rotten eggs mixed with spoiled milk!

Circus Mallet Harley's giant wooden mallet is her pride and joy. It is almost 1 metre long and weighs nearly 7 kilograms. Now that is one dangerous weapon!

The Joker

The Joker is Batman's most dangerous enemy, and Harley's number one role model. She will do just about anything for the Clown Prince of Crime. As she once said, "No one's got more respect for Mister J than yours truly! I love the guy. I really do!"

Harley often calls The Joker "Mister J" and "Puddin'" – but he hates both nicknames!

"Back off, B-Man! You want Mister J, you gotta go through me!"

How much do you know about The Joker?

- Green hair
- Bleached white skin colour
- Hidden electrified joy buzzer
- Acid-squirting flower
- Pop-out knife blades in the front of his shoes

"You know my motto, Harley. If you can't get something at a fair price, steal it!"

The Joker's wacky gadgets

Like Batman, The Joker has an impressive collection of tools. Here are some of the most dangerous:

- Wind-up plastic teeth that explode
- Cannons on the front of his Jokermobile
- Joker venom that causes his victims to smile and laugh uncontrollably
- Razor-sharp playing cards

Dear Puddin'...

Harley loves to leave handwritten notes for The Joker all around his lair. While he almost always throws them away, a few have escaped his waste bin.

Dear Puddin',

I broke into the Gotham City Arts and Crafts shop late last night and stole some wood, glue and paint. Attached is a Batman-shaped dartboard I made just for you. I hope you have fun throwing really sharp darts at it.

P.S. I set off an alarm at the shop, and I think the cops may have followed me back to your hideaway. You might need to find a new place.

Sorry,
Harley

Dear Puddin',

I promise to silence the bells in my cap if you let me go with you on your next caper. I'm sorry they tipped off the cops when we were robbing that jewellery shop last night!

By the way, I saw a diamond bracelet at the shop that would look very cute on me... hint, hint!

Yours truly,
Harley

Dear Mr J,

I'm truly sorry one of my hyenas ate the blueprints for the vault in Gotham City Bank. I don't know if it was Giggles or Crackers, but I guess you could say that they're not paper-trained! Ha! Ha! Get it? Did that make you smile? You know nothing makes me happier!

Sincerely,
Harley

Giggles and Crackers

Have you met Harley's two beloved pet hyenas? Their names are Giggles and Crackers, and they are always hungry. Harley feeds them nothing but the finest steaks, but the hyenas are much happier when they get to take a bite out of one of her foes.

Giggles and Crackers also like to laugh, especially when Harley tells them a joke or clobbers someone with her giant mallet.

How much do you know about hyenas? Take a true or false quiz!

1. Hyenas live in groups called clans.
2. Hyenas are more closely related to cats than dogs.
3. Hyenas are poor mothers.
4. Hyenas are meat-eaters.
5. Hyenas are not very clever.

Answers: 1. True 2. True 3. False 4. True 5. False

The many skills of Harley Quinn

In addition to being a psychiatrist and a criminal, Harley has shown off a few other talents over the years.

Gymnast Harleen Quinzel's gymnastic skills won her a scholarship to Gotham University. She now puts those skills to use by avoiding laser security alarms and hopping down her apartment building's fire escape.

Advice columnist Harley has never had much luck at finding love. But that didn't stop her from taking a job at the *Daily Planet* newspaper in Superman's home city of Metropolis. She had her own romance advice column called Chance@Love!

Member of the Joker's gang Harley Quinn likes to think that she and The Joker are equal partners. The Joker feels otherwise, and he often treats Harley like the lowest employee in his gang. Needless to say, that makes Harley's blood boil.

Boxer Harley once boxed with Superman – and won! The reason for her victory was that Superman had temporarily lost his powers. But Harley never mentions that little detail when she brags about the win.

Punk rock singer Harley went musical – sort of – when she started singing with a punk rock band called the Skull Rags. Wearing a blonde mohawk haircut, she adopted the name of G. G. Harlin for this job.

Super Hero sidekick Every now and then, Harley gives up her criminal career and crosses over to the right side of the law. Determined to do good, she has temporarily worked alongside Batgirl, Black Canary and Batwoman.

I'm ready to be part of the best team ever. Me and my bestie fightin' crime in Gotham City!

Horrible heroes

Gotham City has a host of heroes who make life miserable for Harley Quinn. Here are their secrets!

Batman

Bruce Wayne was only eight years old when his parents were killed by a robber in Gotham City. Bruce vowed that he would grow up to fight crime and later became Batman. Because of his non-stop efforts to put The Joker behind bars, Batman is Harley's number one enemy.

Secret batman facts

His Utility Belt is booby-trapped with an electrical current that shocks anyone who tampers with it.

In addition to the Batcave below Bruce Wayne's home, Batman also has several "mini-caves" around Gotham City.

Batman has several specialised Batsuits, including ones for arctic, aquatic and desert environments.

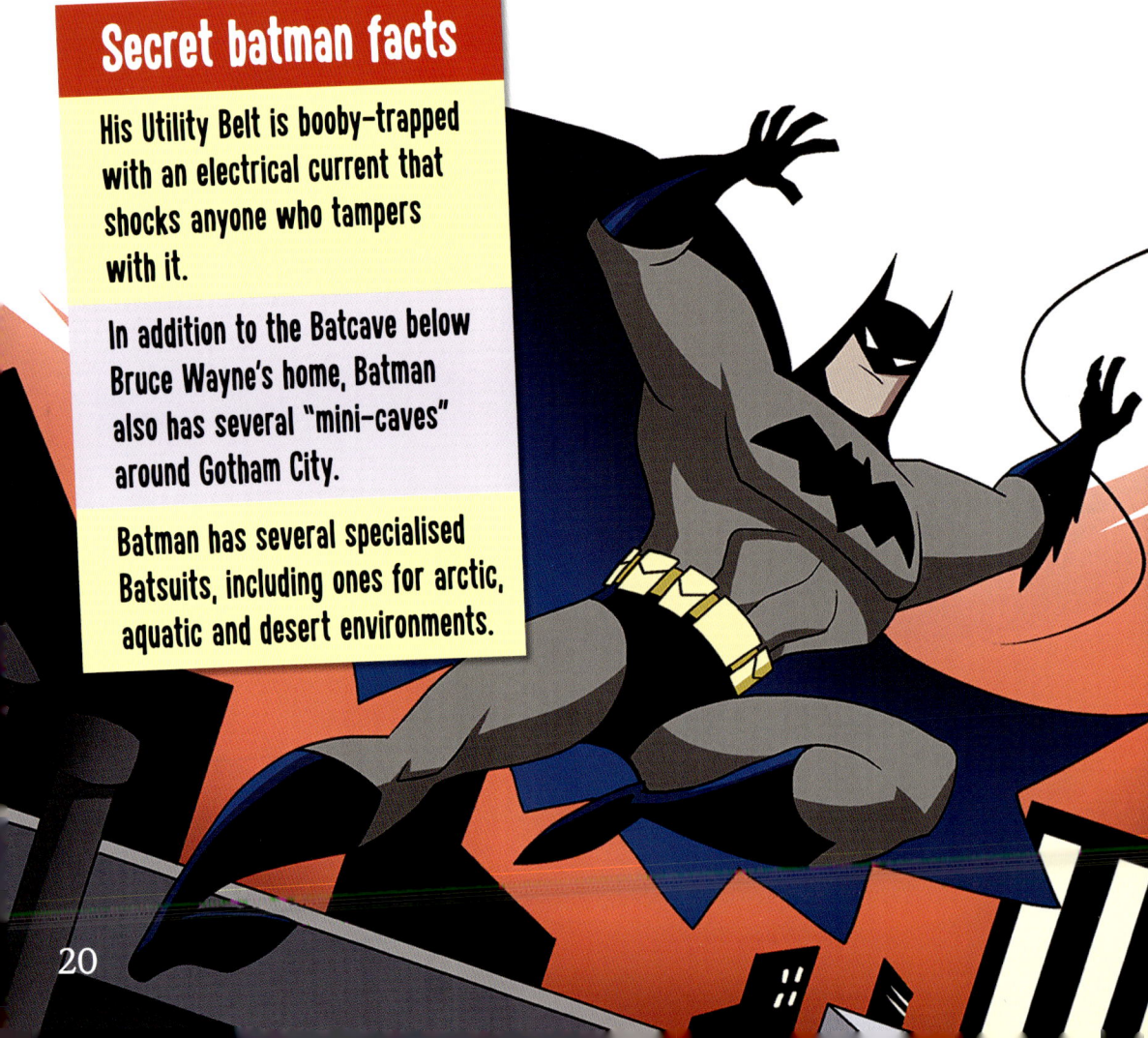

Robin

Two different teens have worn the Robin costume. The first was Dick Grayson. After serving as Robin, he became the hero known as Nightwing. Now Tim Drake boldly wears the Robin costume.

How much do you know about Robin?

1. What is Tim Drake good at using?
2. What is Tim's middle name?
3. What is Robin's favourite vehicle?
4. Who helps Tim with his school studies?
5. What can Robin do with the "R" emblem on his chest?

Answers
1. Computers
2. Jackson
3. Redbird motorcycle
4. Alfred
5. Throw it as a weapon

Sheesh! It's gettin' so a gal can't make a dishonest livin' in this burgh!

Batwoman

After Katherine "Kate" Kane met Batman, she was inspired to wear her own Batsuit and fight crime as the costumed hero Batwoman. Perhaps her strangest mission came when she encountered Harley Quinn. At the time, Harley was feeling depressed because The Joker had kicked her out of his gang – again! So Harley asked Batwoman to help her change from a villain to a hero.

Batgirl

SECRET FILE

- Secret identity: Barbara Gordon
- 1.8 metres (5 ft 11 in) tall
- Utility Belt filled with crime-fighting tools
- Daughter of Gotham City Police Commissioner James Gordon
- Brilliant mind
- Outstanding computer skills
- Expert martial arts fighting skills

Black Canary

Black Canary is an expert martial artist with an amazing superpower. She can vocalise an ultrasonic Canary Cry that flattens foes in seconds.

Are Black Canary and Harley Quinn enemies or friends? It depends on the day. On most days, Black Canary wants to stop Harley's wacky crime sprees. But when Harley is behaving herself, the pair join forces as part of the crime-fighting team known as the Birds of Prey.

Commissioner Gordon

When Batman first arrived in Gotham City, Police Commissioner James Gordon was nervous about working with the masked and mysterious crime fighter. But Gordon soon realized he needed Batman to round up Gotham City's most dangerous villains. Now Gordon is one of the Dark Knight's most loyal friends – and a thorn in Harley's side! He is so serious that Harley sometimes calls him "Commissioner Boredom"!

For cryin' out loud, Harley! Get leads and licences for those hyenas of yours!

Best friends ... forever?

Meet Harley's best friends in the whole wide world ... at least, sometimes.

Catwoman

Catwoman loves to steal anything cat-related: exotic cat-shaped statues, priceless cat-shaped gems and rare felines. She and Harley seem to be best buddies, and they call each other "Cats" and "Harls". But they are often bitter rivals.

Batman will never keep the Princess of Plunder locked up purr-manently!

Real name: Selina Kyle

Occupation: Cat burglar

Outfit: Leather catsuit

Skills: Expert boxer and martial artist

Secret weapon: Retractable razor-sharp claws in gloves

Secret tool: Spring-action steel climbing spikes in boots

Favourite weapons: Bullwhips and cat-o'-nine tails

Rumour: Has nine lives

Poison Ivy

Poison Ivy is Gotham City's Queen of Green. She and Harley are the best of friends . . . most of the time. Harley calls her "Red" because of Ivy's flaming red hair. They have plotted crimes together, fought Batman together and even lived together.

Did you know?
Poison Ivy's powers grow stronger when she stands in bright sunlight and fertile soil.

Ivy's origins

Pamela Isley was a botanist who was born with an immunity to plant toxins and poisons. After some dangerous experiments with plants, Isley's skin itself became poisonous. One kiss from her lips can spread a deadly venom. Taking up a life of crime as Poison Ivy, she now has complete control over plants and flowers, causing them to grow and follow her commands.

Friends or foes?

Gotham City is known for having the most infamous Super-Villains in the world. But do you know which ones have joined forces with Harley? And which ones have sometimes double-crossed her? Here are their secrets!

The Penguin

It was a dark day in Gotham City when The Joker joined forces with The Penguin. And it was a sad day for Harley when The Joker told her that she was not allowed to join the two villains on their next criminal caper. That was bad news for The Penguin because a jealous Harley is a dangerous Harley!

SECRET FILE

- **Real name:** Oswald Chesterfield Cobblepot
- **Occupation:** Nightclub owner and criminal
- **Height:** 1.6 metres (5 ft 2 in)
- **Weight:** 79 kilograms (175 lbs)
- **Favourite weapon:** Flame-throwing umbrella

The Riddler

Edward Nigma is The Riddler. This crafty criminal loves riddles. One time, Harley used her brilliantly bonkers mind to write riddles that she hoped would puzzle The Riddler himself.

Facts about The Riddler

- His question-mark shaped cane can be used as a dangerous weapon.

- He began his life of crime after designing a video game called *Riddle of the Minotaur* that made millions for the manufacturer . . . but not a penny for him.

Killer Croc

When Harley slipped into the Gotham City sewer in search of some valuable blueprints, she tangled with the dangerous monster known as Killer Croc. Luckily, his brute strength was no match for her acrobatic skills. She easily hopped out of the monster's reach.

Sorry, KC. You're going to have to do better than that!

Clayface

During a brief period where Harley teamed up with Batwoman, the unlikely pair of heroes battled the shape-shifting muddy menace known as Clayface.

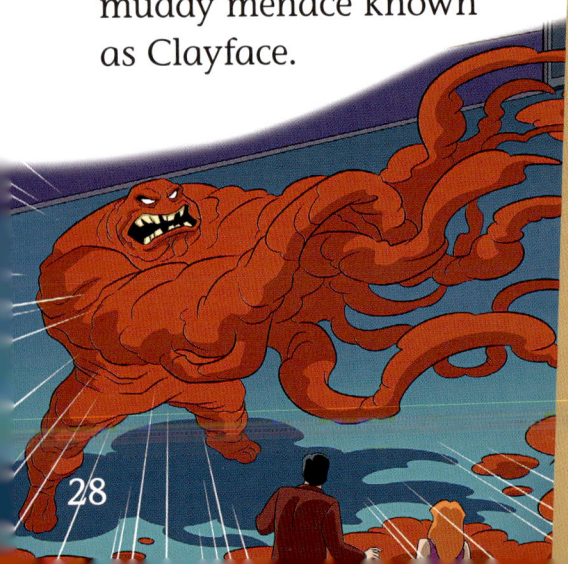

SECRET FILE

- Height: 2.6 metres (8 ft 7 in)
- Weight: 356 kilograms (785 lbs)
- Able to transform into almost anything
- Absorbs the energy of those he consumes
- Can stretch his limbs for long distances
- Able to dissolve into a puddle and disappear into sewers

Bane

Harley keeps her distance from this muscular maniac. But she envies Bane for the one time he defeated Batman in a fight.

Did you know?
Bane is stronger than Killer Croc. Even when Bane's broken arms were bound in plaster casts, he still managed to defeat Croc.

Arkham Asylum

It's the place where Harley worked as a psychiatrist and met The Joker. But how much do you really know about this scary site?

Its official name is Arkham Asylum for the Criminally Insane.

It was founded by Doctor Amadeus Arkham.

The first patient was Martin "Mad Dog" Hawkins, who killed Amadeus's wife.

It was originally designed as a hospital and is now a maximum-security prison.

Many inmates escaped Arkham after a powerful earthquake hit Gotham City.

Historical highlights of the Clown Princess of Crime

- Writer Paul Dini and artist Bruce Timm introduced Harley Quinn as The Joker's helper in a 1992 episode of *Batman: The Animated Series*.

  - Actress Arleen Sorkin gave Harley her voice and an accent of someone who comes from Brooklyn, New York.

- Harley was originally going to make only one appearance on *Batman: The Animated Series*, but she quickly became a favourite of viewers and the show's creators.

  - In 1993, Harley made her first comic book appearance in *The Batman Adventures No.12*.

⚡ Harley got her own *Harley Quinn* comic book in 2000.

⚡ Harley made her live-action debut in 2002 as a character on the *Birds of Prey* TV series.

⚡ Harley made her film debut in 2016 when actress Margot Robbie played the character in the live-action *Suicide Squad*.

⚡ In a 2016 issue of her comic book, Harley got a makeover with a new hairstyle and outfit.

⚡ In the *LEGO® Batman Movie*, Harley's weapon of choice was a large red baseball bat.

⚡ Since her 1992 debut, seventeen actresses have played Harley on TV and in films and video games.

About the author

Steve Korté is the author of many books for children and young adults. He worked for many years at DC Comics, where he edited more than 600 books about Superman, Batman, Wonder Woman and the other heroes and villains of the DC universe. He lives in New York City, USA, with his husband, Bill, and their super-cat, **Duke**.